AF261524

KIDS' REFLECTIONS: SELECTED PRAYERS FROM AS SAHIFA AL-KAMILAH AL- SAJJADIYAH

(UNDER THE GUIDANCE OF
MAULANA SYED ABUL QASIM RIZVI)

ISBN 978-1-7635725-3-9

Published by TS Publications
Truth Seekers Foundation
PO Box 498, Craigieburn, VIC 3064, Australia
www.truthseekersfoundation.org
books@truthseekersfoundation.org

Dear Friends,

Just as we talk to our friends, parents, cousins, and siblings, it's also important to talk to our Creator - Allah (The Glorified). And what better way to communicate with Allah than through the beautiful supplications taught to us by Imam Sajjad (peace be upon him) in his remarkable collection, As Sahifa AL-Kamilah Al-Sajjadiya.

In this book, we'll explore some of these excellent prayers from Imam's collection. Through these prayers, we'll learn how to understand and communicate with our Creator and Nourisher - Allah (glory be to Him).

May these prayers enrich our connection with Allah and bring us closer to Him.

دعاء يوم الأحد

In the Name of God, the All-merciful
the All-compassionate

1- In the name of Allah,
who gives me good things,
and who makes sure things are fair!
I trust only in what He says,
And I hold onto His rope tight!

2- I ask for help from You
(who forgives and likes when we do good)
from bad things and from people who don't like me,
from time passing and feeling sad,
from bad things happening,
and from my time running out before I'm ready.

3 – I ask You to show me what's right and good.

4- I need Your help
with things that will make me successful and happy.

5- I ask You for good health
and to always be safe and well.
Please keep me safe from bad thoughts,
and protect me from unfair people in charge.
Please make my prayers and fasting count,
and make my future better than now!

دعاء يوم الأحد

Keep me safe with my family and friends,
day and night!
Because You are the best protector,
And You are very kind.

**6- O Allah, today and every Sunday after,
I promise to only believe in You and
to never believe in anything else, and
to pray only to You, hoping You'll answer.**

7- Bless Muhammad and his family,
the best people,
who tell the truth about You.
Raise me up with Your help,
always watching over me,
and secure my life with Your forgiveness!
You are very forgiving and kind!

PRAYER FOR SUNDAY

دعاء يوم الاثنين

In the Name of Allah, the All-Merciful,
the All-compassionate

1- I start with praise to Him, who created everything,
He made the sky, the earth, and the souls,
All by Himself, without anyone else's roles!

2- He is the only Allah
and doesn't need anyone else.

3- People can't fully describe Him,
or understand Him completely,
even the powerful are amazed by Him,
and everyone respects His power!

4- So we praise You,
over and over again,
always, in a good way!

5- And may His blessings be on His Messenger forever,
and His greetings last forever!

6- Oh Allah, please make
today start well, be good in the middle,
and end happily!
Keep me safe
from scary starts, worrying middles,
and painful endings!

PRAYER FOR MONDAY

دعاء يوم الاثنين

7- Oh Allah,
I'm sorry for any promises I made
and couldn't keep.

8- I'm sorry if I hurt anyone,
whether they're here or gone.
Please help me make things right.

9- I ask You (who owns everything)
to make the person I hurt forgive me,
and be kind to me!
You're so kind and forgiving!

10- Oh Allah,
on every Monday, give me two things:
the happiness of obeying You at the start,
and Your forgiveness at the end!
You are the only one who forgives sins.

PRAYER FOR MONDAY

دعاء يوم الثلاثاء

In the Name of Allah, the All-merciful
the All-compassionate

1- We praise Allah, it's His right,
He deserves it, lots of praise!

2- I ask Him to protect me from my own bad thoughts,
because without His mercy, my thoughts could lead me
astray.

3- I ask Him to protect me from Satan's tricks,
which make me do bad things.

4- I ask Him to keep me safe from bad rulers,
unfair leaders, and enemies.

5- Oh Allah, put me with Your successful people,
because they always win.
Put me with Your group,
because they are the ones who do well.
And make me Your friend,
because Your friends are never scared or sad.

6- Oh Allah, help me follow my religion properly,
because it keeps my life in order.
Help me do well in the afterlife,
because that's where I'll stay forever,
and I want to stay away from bad things!
Make life good for me,
and make my journey into the next life easy, without
any pain!

PRAYER FOR TUESDAY

دعاء يوم الثلاثاء

7- Oh Allah, bless Muhammad,
the last Prophet,
and his family and friends,
And give me three things every Tuesday:

8- Please forgive all my sins,
take away my sadness,
and protect me from my enemies!
I start with "in the name of Allah,"

9- I want to stay away from things You don't like,
especially Your anger,
and I want to do things You like,
especially making You happy!

10- So forgive me completely,
Oh Allah, who does good things!

دعاء يوم الأربعاء

In the Name of Allah, the All-merciful
the All-compassionate

1- Praise Allah,
who made night like a blanket for us to rest,
and gave us sleep,
and made day for us to wake up!

2- Thank You for waking me up from sleep,
if You wanted, You could have let it go on forever.
I'll keep praising You, forever,
and no one can count how many times!

3- Oh Allah, You deserve all the praise,
You created everything, organized it,
decided how long things last,
gave life and death,
made people sick and healed them,
You rule over everything!

4- I ask You for help,
I'm not very good at asking for things,
I've made mistakes, and I'm sorry.
I'm getting closer to the end of my life,
and I realize how much I need Your kindness.
I feel bad for all the times I've messed up,
and I'm really sorry,
I promise to do better.

PRAYER FOR WEDNESDAY

دعاء يوم الأربعاء

5- Bless Muhammad, the last Prophet,
and his family and friends,
let me be close to him too,
don't take his friendship away from me!
You are the kindest of all!

6- Oh Allah,
please help me with four things on Wednesday:
Help me obey You better,
be happy when I pray to You,
desire Your rewards,
and stay away from things that could make You punish me!
You are kind to whoever You want!

PRAYER FOR WEDNESDAY

دعاء يوم الخميس

In the Name of Allah, the All-merciful
the All-compassionate

1- Praise be to Allah
who makes the dark night go away with His power,
and brings the bright day with His kindness.
He dresses me in its light
and gives me its blessings.

2- Oh Allah, just like You kept me safe for today,
keep me safe for all the days like it.
Bless Prophet Muhammad and his family,
don't let me do wrong today or any other day,
don't let me sin;
give me all the good from today,
and all the good from everything after it;
and keep away the bad from me,
the bad from today,
and all the bad from everything after it!

3- Oh Allah, because I follow Islam,
I ask You to help me!
Because I believe in the Qur'an,
I trust in You!
Because of Prophet Muhammad (Allah bless him and his
family), I ask You to listen to me!
So please, accept my prayers,
I trust You will help me,
Oh Most Merciful!

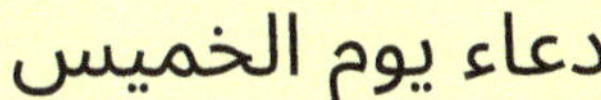

4- Oh Allah, on Thursday, please give me five things
that only Your kindness can give,
and only Your goodness supports:

- health, so I can do what You want,
- worship, so I can get Your rewards,
- enough to live on honestly,
- keep me safe from danger,
- and protect me from sadness and worries!

Bless Prophet Muhammad and his family,
and let my prayers help me on Judgment Day!
You are the most merciful!

دعاء يوم الجمعة

In the Name of Allah, the All-merciful
the All-compassionate

1- All praise belongs to Allah,
who was there before anything existed,
and will be there after everything ends.
He knows everything,
and He never forgets those who remember Him,
never lessens the gratitude of those who thank Him,
He never disappoints those who ask Him for help,
and He never takes away hope from those who trust Him!

2- Oh Allah, I ask You to witness,
and You are enough as a witness,
and I ask all Your angels,
the ones in Your heavens, who carry Your Throne,
Your prophets and messengers You sent,
and all the creatures You made,
that I bear witness that You are Allah;
there is no one like You, You have no partners,
Your word never fails, and You never change;
and that Muhammad (Allah bless him and his family)
is Your servant and messenger;
he told people what You asked him to,
he fought for You as he should,
he gave good news about rewards,
and warned about punishment.

PRAYER FOR FRIDAY

دعاء يوم الجمعة

3- Oh Allah, keep me strong in Your religion as long as I live,
don't let my heart turn away after You guided me,
and give me mercy,
You are the one who gives.

Bless Muhammad and his family,
make me one of his followers,
gather me with him
and help me perform the obligatory acts on Fridays,
and obey You like You asked me to,
and give me the good things You promised for those who do right,
on Judgment Day!
You are powerful and wise!

دعاء يوم السبت

In the Name of Allah, the All-merciful
the All-compassionate

1- 'In the name of Allah',
the word of those who hold tight to Him,
the words of those who ask for His help!
I ask Allah (high exalted is He) to protect me from
the unfairness of mean people,
the jealousy of others,
and the cruelty of bad people,
and I thank Him more than anyone can imagine!

2- O Allah,
You are the One and Only,
and the King without anyone making You the ruler;
no one can change Your plans
and no one can take away Your power!

3- I ask You to bless Muhammad and his family,
Your servant and messenger,
make me grateful for Your gifts
which will make You happy with me,

PRAYER FOR SATURDAY

(on Saturday) help me to be obedient to You,
worship You,
and deserve Your rewards,
have mercy on me,
keep me away from disobeying You
as long as I live,
help me do things that are good for me
as long as I'm alive,
help me understand Your Book,
and make it easy for me to read it,
keep me healthy in my faith and my body,
keep my loved ones close to me,
and continue to be kind to me for the rest of my life,
just like You've been kind to me so far!
Oh Most Merciful!

PRAYER FOR SATURDAY

PRAYER FOR PARENTS

1- O Allah, bless Muhammad, Your servant and messenger, and his pure family, with Your best blessings, mercy, and peace!

2- And please, Allah, honor and bless my parents, You are the most Merciful!

3- O Allah, bless Muhammad and his family, teach me how to treat them well, help me understand what I need to do for them, and give me the strength to do it! Please guide me to do what's right, so I don't forget or find it hard to help them.

4- O Allah, bless Muhammad and his family, You've honored us because of him, and You've given us responsibilities because of him!

5- O Allah, help me respect my parents, like how we respect a powerful king, and let me care for them, like how a loving mother cares for her child! Make me happy to do what they ask, even if I'm tired, and let me care more about their happiness than my own.

6- O Allah, let me speak softly to them, say nice things to them, stay calm when I'm with them, have a kind heart towards them, and be a good friend to them!

7- O Allah, thank them for raising me, reward them for taking care of me, and protect them like they protected me when I was little!

8- O Allah, any harm I've caused them, any mistakes I've made towards them, or anything I owe them, please make it count as good deeds for them, and make them even better people because of it! You are the one who turns bad deeds into good!

9- O Allah, if they've ever said something unkind to me, done something wrong to me, ignored something important to me, or not fulfilled their duties to me, please forgive them, I don't want to be mad at them, or think they don't care about me, my Lord!

10- They've done so much for me, they've given up so much for me, how could I ever repay them? So bless Muhammad and his family, and help me, O Allah, who we ask for help! Guide me, O Allah, who knows everything, not to disrespect my parents, on the day when everyone will be judged fairly.

11- O Allah, bless Muhammad, his family, and descendants, and give my parents the best rewards, like You do for the parents of Your faithful servants, You are the most Merciful!

12- O Allah, help me remember them always, after my prayers, at night, and during the day!

13- O Allah, bless Muhammad and his family, forgive me because of my prayers for my parents, forgive them because of their love for me, be happy with them because of my love for them, and give them a safe place because of Your kindness!

14- O Allah, if You forgive them first, let them pray for me, and if You forgive me first, let me pray for them, so we can be together in Your house, full of Your kindness and forgiveness! You are so generous and kind, You are the most Merciful!

PRAYER FOR PARENTS

Prayer #24 in Sahifa

PRAYER FOR NEIGHBOURS AND FRIENDS

1- O Allah, bless Muhammad and his family,
and help me be good to my neighbors and friends,
who know what's right and stand up to our enemies!

2- Please make my neighbours and friends successful in
following Your teachings,
and being kind to those who need help,
like the sick, or those who need advice.
Help them share with others and be generous,
even before they're asked!

3- Let me be kind to them, even if they're not kind to me.
Let me forgive them if they do something wrong.
Help me see the good in them, and be devoted to them.
Let me be respectful and humble around them,
and help them when they're in trouble.
Even when they're not around, let me care about them,
and wish them well.

4- Oh Allah, bless Muhammad and his family,
and give me the same blessings as them.
Give me a good share of what they have,
and help them see my good qualities.
Let us all be lucky because of each other!
Ameen, Lord of everything!

Prayer #26 in Sahifa

PRAYER FOR WELL-BEING OR GOODNESS

1- O Allah,
bless Muhammad and his family,
wrap me in Your goodness *(Goodness means well-being, health, wellness, contentment, prosperity, happiness)*,
keep me safe with Your goodness,
strengthen me with Your goodness,
give me honor through Your goodness,
make me free from needing anything else with Your goodness,
donate to me Your goodness,
bestow upon me Your goodness,
spread out Your goodness for me,
make Your goodness right for me,
and never separate me from Your goodness
in this life and the next!

2- O Allah,
bless Muhammad and his family,
and give me good health,
a healing that makes me strong,
a well-being for my body,
in this life and the next!

3- Help me stay healthy and safe,
in my religion and my body,
give me understanding,
and help me fear and obey You!

4- O Allah,
bless Muhammad and his family,
and let me visit the holy places
for as long as I live,
make my visit accepted and appreciated by You!

5- Help me always praise You,
remember You, and worship You properly!

6- Protect me and my family from harm,
from every evil thing,
from people who wish bad things for us,
and from creatures that may hurt us!

7- O Allah,
bless Muhammad and his family,
and if someone wants to harm me,
protect me from them,
turn their plans against them,
and keep me safe from all harm!

8- Make them unable to harm me,
keep them away from me,
and keep me safe from all their evil!
You are the most Powerful!

Prayer #23 in Sahifa

PRAYER FOR GOOD CHARACTER
OR NOBLE TRAITS

1- O Allah,
bless Muhammad and his family,
help me to have strong faith,
make me sure of what I believe,
and guide me to always intend good
and do good things!

2- Complete my good intentions,
make my beliefs strong with Your help,
and fix whatever is wrong with me!

3- Bless Muhammad and his family,
keep me from worrying too much,
help me focus on what's important,
and let me live the way You want me to!
Provide for me,
keep me humble,
and help me do good without expecting anything in return!

4- Bless Muhammad and his family,
don't let me become arrogant,
and keep me humble,
no matter what others think of me!

5- Bless Muhammad and his family,
guide me to always do what's right,
and let me live a good life,
but if I start doing bad things,
take me away before I hurt myself or others!

6- Bless Muhammad and his family,
protect me from those who want to harm me,
and help me to be strong against bad influences!

7- Bless Muhammad and his family,
replace any hate with love,
any jealousy with kindness,
and any suspicion with trust!

8- Bless Muhammad and his family,
give me the strength to stand up to those who wrong me,
and protect me from harm!

9- Bless Muhammad and his family,
help me to always forgive,
even when others are mean to me,
and help me to always be kind!

10- Bless Muhammad and his family,
help me to be generous,
to speak the truth,
and to be humble!

11- Bless Muhammad and his family,
give me strength as I get older,
and protect me from doing wrong!

12- Bless Muhammad and his family,
help me to stay away from bad things,
and always choose what's right!

13- Bless Muhammad and his family,
make me think of You when I'm scared or sad,
and help me to always turn to You!

14- Bless Muhammad and his family,
help me to always remember You,
and to do good things for others!

15- Bless Muhammad and his family,
help me to always be fair,
to be kind to others,
and to always follow the right path!

27- Bless Muhammad and his family,
help me to worship You properly,
and to always know what's right!

28- Bless Muhammad and his family,
help me to always do good things,
and to live a good life!

29- Bless Muhammad and his family,
help me to remember You,
to obey You,
and to always do what You want me to do!

30- Bless Muhammad and his family,
give me good things in this life and the next,
and protect me from harm!

Prayer #20 in Sahifa

PRAYER FOR SEEKING REFUGE

1- O Allah, I ask You to keep me safe from
wanting too many things,
getting too mad, feeling too jealous,
being too impatient,
not being happy with what I have, being too mean,
rushing into things too fast,

2- doing what I want all the time,
not listening to what's right,
being sleepy when I should be awake,
doing things that are too hard,
not telling the truth,
doing bad things over and over,
not listening to grown-ups,
trying too hard to be good,

3- wanting to have more toys than others,
not being nice to kids who don't have as much,
not being nice to my pets,
forgetting to say "thank you" when someone helps me,

4- helping someone who's being mean,
not helping when someone's sad,
wanting things that aren't mine,
telling stories that aren't true.

5- Please keep me safe from
being mean to others,
feeling too proud of myself,
and expecting too much from others.

PRAYER FOR SEEKING REFUGE

6- Please keep me safe from
thinking bad things about others,
looking down on kids who aren't as lucky as me,
letting bad thoughts take over,
running out of time for important things,
and being bossed around by others.

7- Please keep me safe from
wasting things,
not having enough of what I need.

8- Please keep me safe from
kids who aren't nice to me,
needing help when I can't do things on my own,
going through hard times,
and not being ready when it's time to leave this world.

9- Please keep me safe from
feeling really sorry for doing something bad,
having really tough times, feeling super sad, having a
bad ending,
missing out on good things,
and getting in trouble.

10- O Allah, bless Muhammad and his family,
and please help us stay away from all these things,
for boys and girls who believe!
You are the kindest of all!

Prayer #8 in Sahifa

PRAYER FOR GOOD OUTCOMES

1- O Allah, You're remembered with honour,
And those who remember You feel strong!
You're thanked, and those who thank You find joy!
You're obeyed, and those who obey You find safety!
Please bless Muhammad and his family,
And help us always remember You,
So every time we think of You,
Say thanks, or do what's right,
We feel good and safe with You!

2- If You decide we need to rest,
Let it be a safe and peaceful time!
And may all the good we've done be clear,
With nothing to worry about or fear.

3- When our lives one day come to an end,
And Your call comes, please forgive us, dear Friend.
Bless Muhammad and his family,
And forgive us for any mistakes we've made,
So we can feel safe and unafraid.

4- On the Day of Judgment, when our deeds are shown,
Please, Allah, keep our wrongs unknown!

5- You always listen when we pray,
And You help us find our way every day!

Prayer #11 in Sahifa

PRAYER WHEN SICK

1- O Allah, I thank You for my good health,
That lets me run and play with joy!
And even when I'm not feeling well,
I thank You for the care You employ!

2- I wonder, Allah, which is better to say,
Thank You for my health every day?
Or thank You for the times when I'm not so well,
When You help me overcome and get better still?

3- When I'm healthy, I enjoy all the fun,
And I try to do good for everyone.
But when I'm sick, it's a time to reflect,
And try to improve, with Your love and respect.

4- So whether I'm well or feeling down,
I know You're with me, all around.
You help me learn and grow each day,
And guide me in every single way.

5- So thank You, Allah, for everything You do,
For the good times and the challenges too.
You're always there, with love and care,
And for that, I'm grateful, everywhere!

6- Bless Muhammad and his family, dear Lord,
Help me love what's good and stay toward.
Guide me through sickness, and show me the light,
And lead me to goodness, day and night.

7- You're kind and generous, Allah, it's true,
Thank You for everything You do!
You're always there when I need a friend,
And for that, I'll love You to the end!

Prayer #15 in Sahifa

PRAYER AGAINTS SATAN

1- O Allah,
we ask for protection from Satan's tricks,
His traps and his lies, which are really sick!
We don't want to fall for his evil schemes,
Or be fooled by his promises, not even in our dreams.

2- Help us not to listen when he whispers in our ear,
Trying to lead us away from what we hold dear.
Keep us strong in obeying You, O Lord,
So Satan's temptations we can swiftly discard.

3- Build a wall around us that Satan cannot break,
And keep him far from us for goodness' sake!
Protect us, Allah, with Your mighty hand,
And help us against Satan's wicked plan.

4- Bless Muhammad and his family, we pray,
And keep Satan's influence far away.
Don't let him trick us or lead us astray,
Help us to follow the right path every day.

5- Make us wise to see through Satan's lies,
And give us strength against his tries.
Guide us, Allah, away from his harm,
And keep us safe in Your loving arm.

6- Keep Satan out of our hearts, we implore,
And don't let him stay there, not anymore!
We want only goodness and light to shine,
So help us, Allah, and make us divine.

7- Help us to recognize Satan's deceit,
And protect us from falling at his feet.
Give us wisdom to know what's right,
And keep us safe in Your guiding light.

8- Bless Muhammad and his family, dear Lord,
Protect us from Satan's cunning sword.
Help us to see through his evil ways,
And keep us safe through all our days.

9- Turn Satan's power away from us,
And don't let him cause any fuss.
Keep him far from our families and friends,
And protect us until the very end.

10- Bless our loved ones and keep them safe,
From Satan's tricks and his deadly chase.
Wrap them in shields of Your divine grace,
And keep them safe in every place.

11- Include everyone who seeks Your might,
And protect them from Satan's harmful bite.
Keep them safe in Your loving care,
And shield them from all Satan's snares.

12- Allah, destroy Satan's wicked plans,
And protect us with Your mighty hands.
Undo everything that he tries to do,
And keep us safe, O Lord, with You.

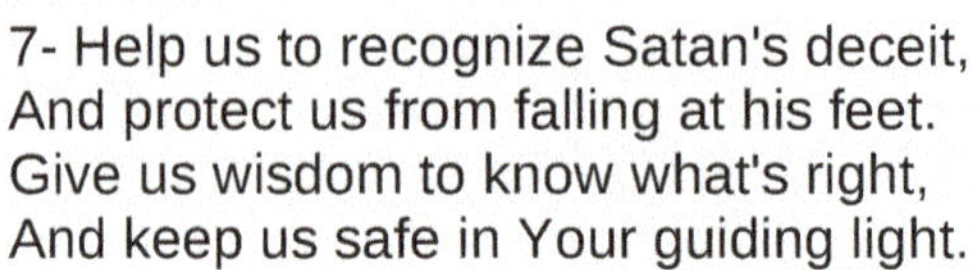

13- Scatter Satan's army, break his hold,
And keep us safe in Your stronghold.
Make him fall down on his knees,
And keep us safe, O Allah, please.

14- Make us enemies of Satan's lies,
And help us against his disguise.
Guide us, Allah, on the path that's true,
And keep us safe, just me and you.

15- Bless Muhammad, our guide and light,
And keep us safe from Satan's might.
Protect us from harm, O Lord, we pray,
And keep us safe every single day.

16- Hear our prayers, O Allah, so clear,
And keep us safe, forever near.
Guide us to righteousness, show us the way,
And keep us safe, O Lord, we pray.

Prayer #17 in Sahifa

PRAYER IN FEAR

1- O God,
You made me just right,
Cared for me when I was small and bright.
You give me what I need each day,
And for that, I thank You in every way.

2- O God,
In Your Book, You say so kind,
Even if I mess up, You don't mind.
You forgive all, You're so great,
I feel bad for what I've done, I can't debate.

3- If it weren't for Your forgiving grace,
I'd feel lost in this vast space.
I know I can't hide from You,
You see everything I say and do.

4- O God,
If I try to run, You're always near,
No matter where I go, You'll always hear.
If You punish me, I know it's fair,
But if You forgive, I'm in Your care.

5- So I ask You, O God above,
Have mercy on me with Your love.
I'm not strong like You, I'm small and weak,
Please forgive me, that's all I seek.

6- Have mercy on me, O Allah, so grand,
Help me, please, to understand.
You're the most powerful, the King of all,
Your mercy is big, it never falls.

7- So show me Your mercy, O God, so dear,
Turn to me with love, calm my fear.
You're the Most Merciful, so kind,
I'm hopeful in Your mercy, I'm in a fix.

Prayer #50 in Sahifa

PRAYER FOR THE REMOVAL OF WORRIES

1- O Helper when I'm worried!
O Comforter when I'm sad!
O Kind One now and forever,
show mercy, make me glad!
For Muhammad and his kin,
ease my worries, lift my sin!

2- O God, You're my shelter true,
not like us, One and Only You!
Guard me well, cleanse my heart,
from all troubles, please depart!

3- Hear my plea, I'm weak and small,
sinful, needy, to You I call!
Grant me deeds that win Your love,
and faith that soars to You above!

4- Bless Muhammad and his line,
let me leave this world in peace divine.
May my heart yearn for Your grace,
and my soul to meet You face to face!

5- I seek goodness, shun the bad,
fearing none but You, my Lord and Dad.
Grant me strength, and wisdom too,
to worship You in all I do!

6- Make my prayers as strong as theirs,
whose faith in You never wears.
Guide my steps, keep me near,
to Your path, O God, make it clear!

7- This is my need, my humble plea,
make it great, O God, for me.
Through it, let Your mercy flow,
and heal my body, make it glow!

8- Some wake up trusting things unsure,
but I trust You, my hope secure.
Guide me right in all I do,
and save me from trials, good and true!

9- Bless Muhammad, guide his way,
and his kin, each night and day!

Prayer #54 in Sahifa

THE TREATISE ON RIGHTS

THE RIGHT OF THE FATHER

The right of your father is that you know he is the reason you exist. He is like the root of your family tree. When you notice something good about yourself, remember that it may come from your father. Be thankful to God for that gift and for giving you your father. Always remember that all strength comes from God.

THE TREATISE ON RIGHTS

THE RIGHT OF THE MOTHER

The right of your mother is that you know that she carried you where no one carries anyone, she gave to you of the fruit of her heart that which no one gives to anyone, and she protected you with all her organs. She did not care if she went hungry as long as you ate, if she was thirsty as long as you drank, if she was naked as long as you were clothed, if she was in the sun as long as you were in the shade. She gave up sleep for your sake, she protected you from heat and cold, all in order that you might belong to her. You will not be able to show her gratitude, unless through God's help and giving success

Right #22